Cathedral of the North

Pitt Poetry Series

Ed Ochester, Editor

Cathedral of the North

Connie Voisine

University of Pittsburgh Press

This book is the winner of the 1999 Associated Writing Programs' award series in poetry. Associated Writing Programs, a national organization serving over 150 colleges and universities, has its headquarters at George Mason University, Tallwood House, Mail Stop 1E3, Fairfax, Va. 22030.

Acknowledgments are located at the end of this book.

For my parents, Myrna and Raynold

The publication of this book is supported by a grant from the Pennsylvania Council on the Arts.

Contents

I

Psalm, *5*

That Far North, *7*

What Grows, *9*

Cameo, *11*

Booming the Lake, *13*

Hungry, *14*

The Dream Was of Her, *15*

In English, *16*

True Stories, *18*

Route One, *19*

Invisible City/Float, *21*

II

The House by the Dump, *25*

Hot, *28*

Hearing, *29*

What Was So Beautiful About the Father, *31*

Rosary, *42*

Invisible City/In the Beginning, *44*

III

Blueberries, *47*

California, *49*

Dirigible, *51*

Ravine, 53

Annunciation, 55

Lemon Ice, 56

Express Dives from Local, 58

Grandfather, 60

Pass the Night, 62

Soloist at St. John the Divine, 64

A Prayer for Final Perseverance, 66

Acknowledgments, 67

"He maketh my feet like hinds' feet, and he setteth me upon my high places."

Psalm 18

Cathedral of the North

I

Psalm

In the morning you are the birds I have no names for,
the birds I do not try to name,
I only triangulate
you, the eye of the bird, flat and shiny,
the eye that finds
the tent of worms, and you are
the worms devouring my tree.

I feel you in the wires in town,
constant, thin, tangled in treetops, black-striping
the blanker pieces of sky.
You are the towers that lift them
legs wide, shoulders ready
to bear what hums a song,
and what a song—a low buzz sprung

from beneath cows and insects,
ash trees and birches weeping their sheets of paper.
Afternoon, you are in my fields
a thousand times. I could say you take the form
of the Red Queen or a silk dress and shoes,
but it is all you, you the sub-
stance, velvet, the raw cocoon,

my deeper pond
where I see you
feeding, a wound in my dark moss.
You are the skin of the pond too, why I want for
microscopes, flush membranes, wheeling

hairs, the infant nub, all that repels light.
You feed my pond

and dusk, you feed my neighbor's hose
        as he washes down his dirty children.
                I know you are the blue in their chests
        as they slip and fall in the driveway,
you say come in now and then it's supper and you
        lay the disappearing road,
the atropine moon.

You are thick and tuned,
        a train's horn shaking windows
                to make them sing too.
        Night, you are the river, your body
clean and cool in this strange city
        and I adore you, fashion
handfuls of your hair into rings,

embroider prayers with the rest. Your
        bank is narrow and populated
                with pilgrims who write their troubles, write
        you on their skins, in rooms,
on the edge of a stamp, the spaces between
        letters blown down airshafts.
From my room, the street promises

in frightening songs and
        your voice is in that radio,
                lips against the bitten sky.

That Far North

I invented my own sign language.
I wrote it down with elaborate descriptions
of the positions of my hands and
where I touched, how I moved them.
The path through the woods behind home
was double-rutted from an old tractor,
abandoned, and I walked in its grooves.
I took out books on flowers,

identified the unbeautiful few that could grow
that far north: mustard, hawk's-eye,
ragwort, and I invented and recorded
for each a silent sign. I found a book
on eating them and began to eat
bark off trees, lick the sap that beaded
on their cuts and buds. I dug up thistles
and ate the roots while my mother,

without my help, cleaned the house
like a woman possessed. *I don't care
how poor you are,* she said, *you can
at least be clean.* The tiny leaves
all around me at the bald top of the hill,
furrowed down to our house.
From up there, I watched the mill lose
its black crown of sparks, and my mother,

big as my thumb at the clothesline,
fought sheets from the wind.

I knew they weren't clean,
she would always work hard,
and each year, the mill rolled enough paper
so it could go, but didn't, to the moon
and back. One of the odd songbirds
half-finished its song. The guide said

these leaves are hardy, adore full sun and
well-drained soil. I picked ten,
rubbed them clean on my pants,
and ate them. Sour. Bright. The sun
slid behind the mill and mouth dry,
I practiced signs to my mother's
small figure, as she began
to mow our acre of lawn.

What Grows

the road a logging road my father (aged fourteen) drove trucks on
    trucks so large they weren't allowed on the normal road
the road scrapes the rim of Soldier Pond where I always thought
    a soldier must have died his bones rotting the water no one
not my cousin Brenda not me would swim in it across the pond
    to Dale's with a lawn of thistles batting the house because
we don't plant flowers *what grows is what grows*
    I plotted to get Dale to come out he was
almost a man thighs tight in jeans we would
    chase each other down past the church St. Cecilia's
a church for the woman who spoke after she was beheaded
    where I would soon go to my first dance and feel
his tongue in my mouth then back to Dale's house where he took
    a branch of thistles and stuck them in my long brown hair and I
took it *sometimes we take it when that's what there is* I pulled
    the husks that wound into my scalp threw them in the pond by
the Babin's blue trailer weeping with rust and their motor boat
    thumping the pier and filled with rain they lost a daughter
in the pond the only redhead in school that brick-colored braid
    in my dreams I lunged for it coming up with hands empty the
        mother works
near mine at a factory sewing zippers or punching snaps on thousands
    of tiny pajamas (this is what women do here) and at our house
the yard blooms with refrigerators and cars insides out and rusting
    my mother's hands look more wrinkled as they fold used
wrapping paper grocery bags tin foil to save (we save everything)
    but the walls are always bare in these houses because *we don't know*
        how
to decorate when I was young I learned if you press your nose

and chin into a bare wall arms stretched out along the chipped
   paint
as if you're hugging it and then if you sing
   your voice gushes back over your face and into your ears
where it doubles and sounds like you're singing with someone.

Cameo

I got good
at finding money in the cracks of chairs,
in heating grates. Once I got enough to slip
coins into the machine and crank it and
a pin, a cameo with a woman's head in
silver plastic on an emerald background
dropped into my palm. She was the most
beautiful thing I owned. Mostly
I hoarded pennies and dimes and traded
the marbles I won or my free lunch cake for

more money. At my Aunt's I saw one, edge
of the counter, the heavy shine of
a quarter, and I couldn't help but take
it when they went to admire her new couch.
I can see the new, clean pink of the pennies
after I washed them in vinegar, then
water, the Canadian ones had leaves on
one side, a queen on the other, and felt
lighter than ours when weighed on the tip
of my index finger. Daily, I opened the money

sock, and my cameo sat on top, pinned
to a satin ribbon which I tied to
my throat. I'd begin counting, that stink
of vinegar and coin, and I was
almost there. On a Saturday my mother
had to go to town, we all went, me and
my little sisters. I gave her the heavy-

toed sock and paid her to take us through
the automatic car wash. Wearing my cameo in
public for the first time, I lay in the wedge of space
above the back seat. I watched the soapy foam
shoot over the window just above my face,
the whips of cloth-brushes spin and
beat me in my box of glass.

Booming the Lake

Goats faint when they hear loud noise, and now their knees
buckle. They fall down dead-like, except one who drags his head over
    their bodies.
The chickens don't care, they stare and blink
white eyelids while the cows jump in their stalls, hooves skate on floors
slick with manure. In the pig cellar the mother pig is screaming,
has begun eating her babies, digging them out of the corners, her
    back working.
The cattails lie flat on the lake, and grandfather, father, uncles and
    police watch,
hands over their ears, elbows making larger, flapping ears. They watch
for the white moon of a child's back to rise in the water, cut loose by
    sound.

Hungry

when I was fourteen I wrote lies to an incarcerated man in
    Florida
lies about my pretty clothes palomino disco records gold rings my
    mother
    bought me he believed me I knew it was a sin but I was so
poor and hated having to eat anything that was free my prisoner wrote
    he wanted to lick my legs slowly like two popsicles down
to the white stick I traded our surplus cheese from the state
    for an electric Lady Shaver and I shaved myself for days
in secret the disco on the radio flooding over my legs I bent I twisted
    touched every inch with the razor the plastic shell buzzed in
    my hand
and numbed my skin while my mother pounded my door
    I was hungry I yelled she kept on pounding *we all are too*

The Dream Was of Her

She tasted her fingers and the salt of
the ocean pulled her back. The curtains
were pursed and the dream was of her, pins

and needles, in the ocean. She had never seen the ocean.
She breathed the water falling off car tires
in puddles, long ones, her mother's
sighs in the hallway as she folded

clothes and her hair was seaweed in her fingers,
tangled in it. She slid a hand mirror
under herself and in the dark she saw the slant,
wet eye.

In English

Did you speak English then?

No.

When did you learn how?

I didn't *learn* anything. As a child I
felt things
in my body.

The shock came later, from the brain,
the naming.

What is it?

I don't know.
It's something
that made me crawl
on my belly, when our house was dark, into my sister's
soaked bed. The smell was awful,
personal. It has a heat. It puts me under.

My mother, in the dark
morning, washed us both.
We stripped ourselves by
the open oven, for warmth.

What is it?

It's not

the water. Once, I tried to drown
some money, some money from
my mother's purse. No, they were food
stamps, they were too
colored. I held them
underwater and twisted and the color
bled into the tub.

What color is it?

I don't know in English.

Don't stop. Say anything.

Surplus sweetened condensed
milk. A baby spoon. Twists of wire
blunting a pig's nose, so many died,
our animals died or sold, I tried
not to grow. Men
could smoke and work—one eye
closed, my father dug hole
after hole for fence posts. After
his accident, the holes just waited.

What exactly happened?

Sometimes it's a leg, sometimes
an eye. I make it a spine sometimes.
A part. It changes.

How is it wounded?

I don't know in English.

Already pregnant, she writes her name and his, Lou and Mike, over
the cloudy pictures in <u>True Stories</u>. Black and white pictures of a
leggy woman (Lou) draped, the arching stem of her throat almost
torn, so thrown back with pounds of hair and a dark man's (Mike's)
kisses. Done eating, Mike scrubs the wishbone from supper and
dries it in the wind on the porch with Lou and her old parents. All
digest and watch cars go by, what happens every night when it's
warmer. Mike gives Lou a leg of the ashy bone. They break it as the
light falls and all color goes away. The parents hoot, *Who won? Who
won?* and Mike takes her shorter piece, says, *This is the man.* He waves
the other part that kept the joint, says, *This is the shovel,* and delicate,
he, in his palm, buries the man with the shovel.

the black man with two plastic legs showed
  up on the Greyhound from
south (everything's south of here) he in his
  wheelchair talked to no one
but himself stayed that whole
  summer at the Fort Kent Hotel fishing off
the Fish River Bridge catching nothing
  that summer of my bike (I always rode
to the bridge always waved at the man
  his orangey legs not the same color
as his arms and face) my cousin returned
  from Viet Nam said they were army
legs my cousin came back a burnt arm
  the same except his mother
cut his meat for him when he was done fighting
  he said he couldn't go anywhere
but here home this last town
  on Route One where you have to stay
you can't just pass through (a dead end
  he said laughing) pregnant our
wild aunt Nat had to marry a man
  from away who stayed (who didn't have
thumbs) I shook his hand at the wedding
  and my hand got lost up his sleeve that
summer I rode my bike around miles
  day and night around the mill
all the time Curly the grave digger
  his fist around the waist
of some liquor barked as he walked around

the store the mill the church
was called Cathedral of the North the man
in a red truck my father didn't know
circled the mill too waved at me and the other one
who came off the bus the
young man in robes (a shaved head)
he stayed at the Fort Kent Hotel
and stood on Main Street (his robes staining
with mud his hair growing in)

Invisible City / Float

Some days she remembers the village as an island
that Gulliver might find,

an island floating in outer space,
an itinerant Rose

Bowl barge made with six hundred
thousand hothouse roses and

wire, tape. Roses of holy influence, she insists
sometimes. The village is tethered to the ground by cables

of metal, twisted by wind
and rocking heavy with land.

A gigantic pendulum defies—
it's bound, it's

flight. She remembers best the sweating
selves who watched the tethers and monster posts keeping

the village reined in. They steer the island clear of satellites,
asteroids, storms, without charts or sextants,

guessing from the smog at sunset or
the thickness of the pelts of dogs and caterpillars.

The workers do eat
richly. They eat

turkeys stuffed with truffles, sauerkraut,
tureens of lamb masala, they eat

waiting, like monks or pregnant women, unable to do more,
no longer of this world or any other.

The only sound is one of crying, as she describes
it, the way a ship cries, against its ropes.

II

The House by the Dump

The middle son drives 40 miles
to get me, in a truck
spotted with bottles and hay
and tools, and a quilt he,
unashamed, spreads on the seat,
his big dog hand creeps over the wrinkles
and I sit where he pats.

A day moon is cut by the barn roof.
The largest garden I ever saw,
here are the pigs, and the dogs,
Pa is the dog warden, and
the miniature dandy hens
with their little yellow eggs,
and there are some brothers,
7 in the house (minus
the four married or dead),
Joseph, kicked by a horse,
and Pee Wee and Blanc and
June, his name is Joseph too,
and the horses.
Here is Star, his horse,
He jumps on bareback,
I'm laughing, Star is bucking,
his hands are waving over his head.
I take a picture,
one that I still have
in a silver frame,
then he bounces into the mud.

Four brown girls sit in a row
on the porch, eating boiled potatoes
with sugar. Manon will sing for me
but I can't look. Facing the dump,
I hear a voice
like a spider touching me all over.

His mother Antoinette Marie
fixes us plates and sets us
chairs close to each other.
He says want some water?
It's delicious.

What about a well near a dump?
My mother washes my knees
with Brillo on Saturday nights
after we say the rosary with the Bishop
on the radio, "Notre Pere qui est en cieux . . . ."
The clean corners of my house
are serious,
where girls always wear slips
and don't sweat and weaken
with boys in trucks or barns
or anywhere.

He leaps up and pumps, muscles
curving like wood,
and the water seems to pour
from high up.
The little girls are pulling me,
shimmying, singing,
good water, good water.

He gives me a glass,
the dump smoke curls in pigtails
against the windows, I know
I will marry him.
His big hand is wet,
glass gently in it,
his eyes blue
like tunnels to the sky.

Hot

He eats in silence as frost plumes at the panes and stars tighten
to teeth marks on the freezing sky. His boots stand in snow water,

melting by the wood stove he burns hot to husk his legs of cold.
The fire bumps, drops, cracks in it. His wife and daughters'

talk goes louder then softer, in and out of the raw, raw
of the chainsaw still in his head where he fells trees that moan

before they drop, mute. First his legs hurt in the snow,
and then his heat loosens the ice in his beard and as he prunes

the fallen trunks, he opens the zippers his wife sewed into his pants
across the thigh, behind the knee, like slits in a pie. The trees

don't bleed in winter. Sap pulls back to the core.
He rises, shudders a crowbar through the slender iron doorway

to the red flare inside.

Hearing

His pulse beats him
like a broom, the man sitting in
the circle of blood, red
wicking through the white
snow. He has one eye
closed, the other spread
into his palm.
The chainsaw chokes,
stalls still in the jagged
woods glinting ice like teeth.
Dark grows between the trees.
In the silence he hears the snow
first crack, then rustle like suds
in his baby daughter's hair,
her fat legs straight in the kitchen sink
her feet pointed,
stiff as fish
before he pours a cupful
of water over her silky
skull. Steam lifts
from the snow in curling feathers
that float from his body. The circle
of blood deepens. He wants to buy
his daughter a horse. He sees
its muscled chest flicking
as it canters on the path under
the power lines. She is making
talk by the shift of hips, rubbing heels,

her fingers loose on his bridle
over a rippling jaw, her fingers
soothe the long tube of his ear.
Her whispers trickle in.

What Was So Beautiful About the Father

My memories are the kind janitors
sweep up from cutting room floors, scraps—
        an expression in a woman's lips not meaningful
enough, an odd shot of shoes,
        the before and after, but not the moment itself.

I remember him red-faced
carrying slop pails to the pigs
        and on his back the oyster-white brace
is bright in the August sun,

        pale moths balanced above him, waterlogged
by humid air, the fussy buckles
        of a too-clean back brace,
incongruous on a man like him.

My mother slaps my face, "You're selfish."
My four-year-old sister
        disappears for a day
and he shouts her name, shuffling his small steps.

Food from the Parish of the Holy
Family, animals sold few by few,
        a bandage over my father's eye, baseball-sized,
snowy, the visible injury, the minor one.

He had two before I was born, the subject of many a story where,
heroically, he is hurt beyond belief. The first was the most spectacular,

though I only have his version, and his truth has a different life. He told us stories of how logging companies paid the men with baloney and sugar. How in the camps, loggers wore the same, lice-ridden, long wool underwear all winter; they'd turn them inside out a couple times a day to relieve itching. Their wives burned all work clothes in the spring. Information that was absolute, the past was magical and true, more colored and exotic. It had an air of the tragic, if only because its result was the dull, difficult way we lived now.

My father was 18 years old when the catch on the gate of an empty logging truck fell open, trapping his head against the metal fender. He doesn't remember pain; in fact, he pulled himself free and stumbled towards the cabins where the other loggers had begun lunch. His own father found him first. He looked at his son and said, "Christ, tu vas mourir" (you're gonna die). The logging camp was hours from any paved road. The story finishes with an Indian logger, some trick with spider webs, and a plane unexpectedly landing on the lake to deliver fireworks and whiskey for Fourth of July.

Before his rescue, my father said to the men gawking at him, "I'm thirsty." His father ran to get a glass of water from the Cooky, and my dad drank it. He said he felt the water fall through the bottom of his jaw and spill onto his chest.

Springtime, there was a flood.
In the psalms, King David lists,
                    as a way to praise Him,
                    all of God's great

destructions. God shakes the cedars of Lebanon,
strips forests bare.
                    He rides enthroned
                    upon the waters of the flood.

Our floods, hungry, omniscient,
were indeed

   such a throne.
   We heard the river buckle and crack,

It swallowed Main Street, filling
stores, cars and the church, water
   of a sparkling,
   diamond texture,

damage still a matter of imagination,
memory. Some clung
   to their roofs and waited
   to be rescued from the air.

Benign flood, almost, because so dependable.
We all knew the most tragic things
   become benign
   with enough repetition.

  A photograph of my father's second accident: the dump truck's cab is flattened and its body impossibly twisted. The story of this accident was not told as often, since, being an expert storyteller, my father knew the events were too standard. The truck, with my father driving, his German Shepherd in the passenger seat, barreled down a narrow road near New Sweden—a twenty-foot drop on one side of the road and a few cars coming toward it on the other. A train crossed the road at the bottom of the hill as my father's brakes went out. It was then he made the choice to go off the drop. He broke some bones and was badly bruised; the dog was killed. My parents had just begun dating at that time and my mother, a shy high-schooler, was overwhelmed with compassion for him. She also knew that his money, even though he was 22, went to his family. The drama of this man can still pierce her.

Because my father's accidents were
inevitable they cease to be a tragedy
in the modern sense.

Logger's homes are filled
with the wide shiny scars of sawed
knees, burned fingers, the unhealable

joints, broken backs—I should know better
to think the last one a disruption. The ancient
idea of tragedy is more appropriate

to some people's lives—the hero, doomed
by himself, his faults and fate. Tragedy is in
the unbearable execution,

in his realization that escape
is impossible. I knew all my life
that anything gorgeous would therefore

be doomed, another unassailable equation.

Many people know you can live, and even work off and on, with a
    broken back.
Many know what it means to a family when its spine has been broken.
Many know the exhaustion of public assistance.
How fear can pretend it is pride.

How deeply unreasonable the notion of an omnipotent god seems at
     these times.
Many know how it feels to be bred to a profound, eventually source-
     less sadness.
How that makes the sadness unspeakable.
Many know what it sounds like when your father with a broken back
     walks stiff-legged down the stairs in the middle of the night to
     lie on the living room floor as if he were lying on a blade.
Some know, as snowplows crease the road, that you should burrow
     deeper into the blankets on the couch. Fake a dream so you can
     turn away.

A movie I remember from my childhood opens with a dreamlike
version of the ordinary: construction workers eat sandwiches from metal
lunch boxes, their large hands delicate around the cups that are the covers
to their Thermoses. They plan for the lives of their children with certainty,
quiet enthusiasm and love. Later, digging, they discover a buried vault,
covered with strange hieroglyphs. The workers ask each other in awe *who
put it there? what power strong enough? why inside this town?*

In the vault they find large grasshopperlike bodies covered with
ooze and coming to life. Their heads are rounded, childlike, limbs jack-
knifed against their bodies. Their eyes are brilliant. Black. I loved these
grasshoppers for being all eyes, for those blacknesses the size and shape of
drumheads, as if any minute now they would start beating. I can still see
their bodies shake.

A workman takes a grasshopper-alien in his arms for a closer
look. The earth's core gives off heat, so he wears only a thin, white T-shirt.
He is the man who earlier insisted that the world is getting better with all
these changes in the space age. Now, he is brave and tender with this alien

being. We see his knees start to weaken, his head fall back, throat dirt-creased, a spire. Like the soldiers who wear cloth jumpsuits against A-bombs, he falls dying too, in the glory of doing his job. Meanwhile, the creature is the one who is terrified, I believe. The creature is the one who must fly from the man's arms to explain everything.

In springtime, in the flood, I stand on icebergs
        in a lake of cellar water. I love to make leaves
slip the currents, to send armadas of
        sticks down the pump's pour, my fingers blue.
Trucks left rusting in this field beside
        our house are silent, hulking
dinosaurs that smell like iron. Each bubble
        in the lake is my subject, one I can slay
with a touch. Sometimes, I announce that I am
        their ruler, rubbing my whiskers. My voice is large,
belly first, arms wide, voice booming.
        Being king involves also much irrational
destruction of my subjects, best carried out alone.

Those glorious aliens consort
with my idea of power in an instinctual way.
In my small scrap of world, my father is
fragile as those bubbles and cannot withstand
fate and evil, equivalents.
Being poor is my father.
A Russian doll series, the largest
is this Evil, and it encloses the doll of Poor.
My father is the next doll, he
disappears into Poor while completely containing

me. I am lucky, the smallest doll
whose features are plain, barely articulated
by the brush, the one whose body won't
open. Who can't bear that she is the reason
the others' sturdy, wood torsos have split.

Spring is as difficult as winter. The ice cracks with a subterranean shudder. Its surface becomes sweaty and dark as its frigid mantle thins. There are the jokes and bets about when it will happen; people remember who got tricked by the ice in 19—, their ice fishing cabins, cars or snow-mobiles sinking into what, the day before, seemed as dependable as the new road to Ashland, or the neighbor's dog that barks all night. The priest fell in one year, his Lincoln Continental burping its way down below what had been, only yesterday, a shortcut across Eagle Lake.

People do die from these mistakes of judgment. Frankie Michaud's brother didn't make it. They found his body after his friend struggled to shore. In his frozen clothes, the survivor wandered into the road and found help, but it was too late. Dana Beaulieu's suicide after forty-nine years of taking care of her alcoholic parents, younger brothers and sisters, and then her own illegitimate child, I am sure, was inspired by the breaking ice. After two weeks of listening from her window to the siren song of Frankie's release—"it was so cold, his heart stopped immediately," "there's nothing you can do once you're stuck under the ice," "the river is so strong when it's high," "I bet he didn't feel a thing"—Dana probably began dreaming in a way she never let herself before. Dana left her car (finally paid for) by the mill, left it with the key in the ignition and the door open.

I don't let myself imagine what it would feel like to die in the river
            during
        spring but I know those

six month winters. Darkness, cold so sharp it paralyzes cilia in your
        nose, how
    sometimes, any exposure at all
means frostbite. The skies are seldom clear, and when they are it's
        because
    the cold is more extreme.
I think clouds are a blanket to hold in whatever heat escapes our
        houses, our
    cars, our puny
bodies, and now, that brilliant blue means something dangerous. We
        receive
    what the sky really wants for us.
It doesn't take long before you can tell how cold it is from your
        window,
    from how the exhaust
from cars hangs in stiff curls from the lips of tailpipes. The spruce
        grow especially blue-black,
    and the ghost-arms of the birches break with a touch.

  I did not know when I was young that the science fiction movie's
beauty had something to do with the 1950s, California and the middle
class. To me, the cars were voluptuous and winged; their shining grillworks
transformed their approaching forms into beings with complicated, or-
nate faces, faces with four eyes and mouths of arching chrome. The houses
were not mundane or uniform. They were seductively perfect. The shrubs,
living plants, were clipped into the shapes of fences or of gifts yet to be
opened. Some ambitious-with-a-shears neighbor might secretly crave a
dolphin leaping from his emerald lawn, but in that world he kept it to the
backyard, within the barnyard fence, by the statuary bought at the local
garden center. He trimmed his topiary on Saturdays, and struggled to keep
the dolphin's delicate nose tapering, yet full. This was not for the front

lawn, this struggle. He would not spoil the deck of cards feeling, the slices of bread aura of his town for anything.

The girl I was longed for this purity. That's why, in the movie, the contamination of the water supply was so devastating. Standing hip against the counter, the father of a family took a few draughts of water, done mowing the lawn, polishing his car, whatever luxurious task—I had no real idea what that kind of father would do on a Saturday. I did understand that, after chores, he only wanted a long, cool drink of water. I would have gotten it for him. One thing I did understand is how hard a father worked, how little it amounted to, and how forgiving I had to be because of it. Whatever anger and helplessness I felt were nothing compared to his when he came home and knew he was not providing well. If he wanted water, he got the coldest water.

On the fragile shoulder
of the road, culverts flow
with runoff so cold you can't
see through. It's oil-slick,

opal-like. I know you've
held water in your hand,
felt cold ache like that, haven't
you? Skin is frictive with the

universe of things,
holds memory in its mesh
of pervious-celled nerves:
too-small shoes pain

the feet, the bald hills, raw,
bear their disfigurement

better. But isn't this a sort
of rapture, not the water,

the valley, but you and
me—that now we both see
land, feet, and *opals somehow
white,* that we agree there is

no opening like the mouth,
and now I sing for you:
*the sky is blue, a sheer,
fragile cuff and the spire's*

too slender for its wrist.
Memory permanently
scored, internal, is in
our skins—take off

your shoes, touch the water.
It's cold enough to stop
your breath. How blue the veins,
your whole body a wrist.

My sister calls it "working too close to the stump." The farther away from
the stump you are, the more of a chance you have to make it. The mill
owner makes more than the equipment store man who makes more than
the chainsaw repairman who makes more than the man who cuts the trees
down.

Too close to the stump.
A declaration against the physical—
        my father's stumped body too connected
to his livelihood. To criticize
        my father's lack of options
and the result, a broken body,
        is to criticize the main expression of his love
for us. He worked his health into ruin,
        worked harder than he could and in my mind
this sacrifice is impossibly tangled up
        with my notions of what love is,
a carnal expression, fraught
        with complications, and always threatening
to break.

Rosary

There is a fort left over from a bloodless war.

There are dogs sleeping, ribs still.

There are animals running deep half-moons at the ends of their chains.

There are chainsaws that gnaw at the other side of the hill.

There are hoses dancing tight with water.

There is a grandfather with a mouth.

There is a grandmother who has none.

There is a doll, the door in her back rusted open, voice box spilling out.

There is a dump, smoking on the top of a hill.

There is no gift for the bride.

There are shoes that are given and are too tight.

There is bath water we share.

There is dust on their wings that makes them fly.

There are flies that eat the part in a girl's hair.

There are jars of carrots, beets and tongue.

There are no benches for the widow and her children, for the Indians, for the cripple.

There are Sears catalogues four times a year.

There are the handmade dresses.

There is the moose who ruined the truck and the truck's pieces.

There are the black-handed uncles and cousins.

There is what we desired, but mostly what we got instead.

There is a spool used as a trumpet, a handkerchief for a veil, a pail for a cage.

There is a weed we can eat.

Invisible City / In the Beginning

Glaciers dragged their ribs
against the mountains creating
and the pines grew extreme,
black knives against a moon.
Fire was
a tether to the sky
and the ocean lugged itself
around and dinosaurs
ruined its once delicate shoulders.

Wandering commenced.
The bears who came
got smaller and rangy,
so was it that loons
only speckled the silence
settling
low-heeled, cloudy,
while mercenaries straggled
down river

entering between
Quebec and Massachusetts.
They grew tubers and ate
what they killed, watched the snow
eloquently remove
what they forced
from its spare face. They believed in
but did not trust
a son of god, that wounded figure.

III

Blueberries

No steady wonder, but revelation
a jolt and my limbs feel silk
weeping a hand's deep tremor before
it's pulled off an electric wire
because you didn't hear the low drone warning
driving I see a car's twisted grill feel
the soft thud
of my own body sagging over the steering wheel
metal making St. Sebastian of
me my wounds the hem of my shirt lifted
in ecstasy—sometimes a gentle
knife slits the top
of a pie sometimes it's a gush my retarded cousin
and her twin boys or old
Abelard who pays children to buy milk and bread
when he can't get out
I lean
into it
noise like a heel in the head something bright
and switching layers
move against layers skin muscle liquid
liquid drips into the throat and stills there
pooling everything gone again
before I can breathe

Then I go home
I no longer
have the luxury of imagining the ways

the world is full
I know how full
A high like
too much speed
when seconds bloom and
hair feels like straw the summer
I picked blueberries
on the barrens I ate speed like candy
and sometimes still
my nose fills with that heavy purple and the weight of sun
calms me.

California

I walk west down the street,
reading *love, Jan, O Positive,*
filigreed, cut in surfers' skins
with animals—an impossible scarlet
tiger stuck clawing its way up a man's shoulder
and indigo birds wing to wing
a limb. The precarious
flower is the one that opens
on the slope of the girl's chest who leans
in a doorway, bare feet. The precarious one
is me and the tree in my old yard
in California, its long trunk spare
and thick. Rats rustle in its crown
and in my ear;
I go to the end
of the spindled pier, stretching over the sea
where whole families catch their suppers.
Grandmothers luxurious in nylons and hats
eat candies slow. Men flip
the cold Blues to thrash in buckets.
The waves get wilder.
I spit over the rail
and don't wait to see.
The nibs of gulls write us
and boys

with the poised bodies of penny-soldiers
slip through foam, ride

gravity and the moon
shoreward,
ankles tethered to their boards.

Dirigible

We met at the Air Show.
You were not upstaged by the Colonel's Machines,
they flew in such formations,
inches between wing-tips, there was a voluble
evil in the woosh I felt in my lungs,
in the loop-de-loops left behind
as smoke. You
linger in my mind, tethered to the steeple,

the radio tower, or to the
tree house where a lone forest ranger watches the horizon
for fires day and night
which never come.
This is a wet land, as you
must already know, my fat, helium,
dreaming boat,
our cows survive winters of bitter cold,
our fires get fed, and we
are easily terrified
by noise or smoke.

I, too, watch the sky
but it's always for you—I know one day
you'll lumber over the hill's cleft—pregnant, silent
you. Meanwhile,
events do not shatter, the earth
is cut regularly for crops.
Only hawks and the odd
grackle break up the sky

with earthly
kinds of heat, a susceptibility to gravity.
I unfold myself on the grass
in my backyard and wonder
are there many other things like you
who also fly without having feet?

Ravine

Long and thin, he was the loudest and
drunkest there, I knew it would be easy,

proximity—enough. He stumbled
out with me and we found the dike.

I feel so good he shouted, feet planted. The river
was flat, unmoving, so full was it.

Black spruces on the Canadian side waited
like cattle, large and familiar as I turned

to him and the stars were thick as salt spilled for the trees
to lick. My body hummed, face to the Border,

and I began not so much a
going away but a moving into. All membranes

inflamed—trees, water, his boots,
my hair on my back—his voice

intruded, but only to narrate, to provide
a shape, metaphor. *I feel so good, I could beat*

the whole world up he said and I saw it,
arms, legs and heads lined up on the dike

like flowerpots, glittering units of flesh appearing
because he said it. Down the road,

I said what he made me see, those parts on the dike,
and he whooped, fists above his head, fell

down into the culvert. Later, he revealed
his Paratrooper tattoo, swirled pastels

for the parachute's silk, a tiny black figure tight
on black ropes, angled into the crook of his arm,

towards his smooth chest. Where his
biceps met the rib cage was a dark

crease, a ravine, another secret.

Annunciation

Tight as a birthday balloon held between palms,
your flesh became an odd crinoline.
Was it on Market Street? George Street? Or on the plain grid where
your house is now?
The book's perfume lifted as you touched it: must, dead clover,
wood smoke.
No, your flesh became the silk of slips, stockings, limpid, luminous.
You say nothing about it
but the airport speaks for you—
the negative whoosh shakes the fruit trees, the clotheslines quiver
and speak too while a cat groans with her painful heat.
Rust.
The wine of your calling burns the nose first, then tongue, throat.
The bone of your calling slipped from an angel who asked
difficult questions of your skin.
(It was saying yes.)
You were told you would never die, that it would be
unnecessary.
The robins were called God's birds since they ate nothing.
Remember?
They fell from your hands and flew in the folds of the sun, wind.
The book opened more, like a pomegranate.
Many blood-red bursts and the grit of seed.

Lemon Ice

for M. H. S.

You are better
than the lemon ice
I had on the
street, the man's
arched knife
shaving a groove
in a block of ice
that sweats, takes my
slow breath, moist
in this heat
which stops wind,
a leg looks luscious,
a biceps curves
like a smile with
salt in it,
and people are in
the fountain, a dog
lunges at the spout,
brindle fur slick
on his body,
teeth biting
the fat stream
from Neptune's mouth,
a baby tumbles under,
pants heavy
with water.
The man spills
the bright flavor

into my cup.
The paper cone
is loose, dissolving
in my hands so
I bite the ice,
filling my mouth,
sharp lemon stings
my lips, makes water
in my eyes, my thirst
absorbs the melt
and my tongue rolls
in sugar. You are
better than that.

Express Dives from Local

Still you want to slip in sideways, largely
        unnoticed by the Haitians, who once sold you
cigarettes and milk. St. Patrick is the store's name,
        green outside and in, the family spelling each other
in their diamond box, bulletproof, waves of TV light
        splashing up the walls and over your hands. Money

pushed through a narrow aperture, a hole for sound,
        for breathing. The street tar purples at night. You forgot how that
slowly happens, how it passes through gray first. You walk
        on purple, streetlight pooling on corners
and before buildings where ex-junkies look out
        their clean windows, stripped to the bone, waiting

for something. They must miss that automatic
        desire, feel it in their mouths and arms. This sidewalk
feels more than familiar, and down in the subways, the trains pass
        almost colliding. The night air thickens with whispers
from their long throats, *A fragment, A figment, The longest*
        night is coming, Hundreds of newspapers under my wheels,

The tracks are hot and quick, my brakeman, my driver.
        Express dives from local with a movement too urgent
to be graceful. This speeding body is weak against the flood
        of words covering the tunnel walls, words full of people,
love, intentions. The Sicilian woman (how could she
        be eighty?) said her father built this line and that's why

her coffee shop looks so familiar, why you come here so often—
    not the deep booths, but the same hexagonal tiles, over years,
few by few brought home in pockets or lunch pails.
    You know I can't stop working, she says, *what am I*
going to do, this is my home. Imagine, over years, the mass
    of tiles hoarded in a cellar corner, a safe,

cool box overflowing. You want to carry gold ones home
    in your mouth, smooth side to your tongue. How it must feel
when you lay them on the floors and walls of a space
    in figures of pyramids, words, the wings of a bird.
Rough pieces of a city materialize, crossed by clouds.

Grandfather

Is this where we end? The 5:00 a.m. call, my bed
where I cried, weak, until 7, are your last words

to ask the nurse *please find out what kind
of tractor is tearing up outside?* Was it when

you pulled me to the garden's far corner
to see an odd patch of grass, grown

impossibly fine? *Here, take your shoe off,*
you said, *never find it soft as this.* How do I

close that household we keep inside my brain?
In cities they're vague, but home these stars

pierce from mill to the luminescent screen
of the drive-in, to the steeple, to hills. I know stars

have lives in other places—I've followed a eucalyptus'
bone-white arm upward, found this same star,

resting on a branch, a ring on its hand.
Here, the maples, black and snow-mossed,

have dropped their teeth, skirts, loose hairs,
in that ritual detaching. As a kid, you lost

your pinkie to a saw, cutting the lake for ice,
and your glove remained whole. (I loved to yell

when you wagged the blunt finger.) Do
stars die cracked like ice dropped in tonic

or do they break, as if sawed, with more precision?
Is anything that neat, that known? Even the lake

is bottomless in places, you said.
A satellite races through the empty treetops,

through Orion's hair. The prophet commands, *lay sinews*
upon me, and I see a celestial army waiting

to rise. Is this you in your fineness?
I never fought anything this large.

Pass the Night

Passe la nuit, we said,
as if we were coffee cups upside-down in the cupboard,
breathless for morning, as if we were
burdocks, the tall green ones
formal for the moon, aloof to wind
and rats on their furtive paths
to the garden.
               We passed the night
or it passed us—thick cream poured from jar
to cup to cup, and away,
a smaller trembling in each lip.
               We went to bed and passed the night,
not in French or English, and night was
our Lourdes, our Calvary, our house,
the cat, the dog,
everything resurrecting
night's dark city in the creases
of bed sheets, mysterious swaddling city.
               Gone. *Into the night*
we passed, as into our grandfather's eye,
bottomless, brimming the fields,
and into his smoky throat. He coughed
and died, left the night alone
to shake with its singleness,
               silence. *We passed the night.*
We were translucent, night kissing
the bed through us, running its thorns through
to the floor. We were these mountains
before they mapped them, before

we dreamed of them, before the
first mother knew, filled with Abel. Please
   pass the night in peace, no
restless tossing, angry
knocking on its damp door. The night's peace, its
chrism, its oil, that shifting
rainbow inside closed lids
and the uncle who fell drunk into snow.
   Pass the night safe at home,
we prayed. The night that was jewel or
fern—fisted, unknown.

Soloist at St. John the Divine

Cutters each day separated stone
from the narrow feet of the Virgin. This curve
of thigh, the cloth sculpted, all draped
in resignation, frozen, they predict their end.
Marble gestures of a body, a death.
Blue veins feather a hand permanently,

failing as I do here. The soprano offers me
a different hand, one too vivid, her mouth,
rigid around each word, holds a dark
strait of sound. Her high note sends snow
off the eaves, then a wreck of silence settles
on my coat and hands, returning me to myself.

If only permanence required a pulse,
then the widening of the singer's throat, her
tongue at her teeth, the velvet sleeve of her legato
would be too mortal to perish. One short bone, sensitive
to air, shakes with the weight of song and cuts
its own music in my brain, unfurling response,

these worries—*why, death, beautiful singer.*
Hard pebbles fall in the spaces between sounds.
A crown of stone roses encircles a beast
scowling from high in an arch, ugly,
humanlike. His, painstakingly accurate,
is the shocked face of a bat. Does he bemoan

the cutter's hands that made him
eternal without the soprano's tremble?
His expression is more difficult to read.
He tells me with his carved mouth to trust
the cutter's logic, the gorgeousness of stone

is that it sings back, even if "in the figure of"
does not mean real. Silent and sending back
her voice over hundreds of years, he too dissolves
under a smaller, more restless tool, says
the imperishable is us, like stone, always growing
smaller, is the famine inside any song.

A Prayer for Final Perseverance

Snow drives and is folded into
the cornerless, edgeless town and in the absence
    of day, snow is light—plows fold it into the road.
Snow spills from my legs and if I keep walking it will cease being
    toward, I will violate less. The weave of my
wool coat loses itself to shags of snow
    while windows offer up jewels: a turquoise TV sea
lulls people to sleep, furniture fitting their bones,
    a boy dreams to an animal light glowing in a socket,
a woman heats then swallows milk from a mug
    with a gold crest of arms. Steam curls
from my wrists and face, and tonight the stars
    are accounted for and there's a distance in which
all of us are born sinless, each
    in lit windows, silent rooms.

Acknowledgments

The author and publisher gratefully acknowledge the following publications, in which some poems in this volume previously appeared: *Seneca Review* ("In English"); *Ploughshares* ("Hot," "True Stories"); *Phoebe: A Journal of Literary Arts* ("What Grows"); *The Threepenny Review* ("Hungry"); *The Cream City Review* ("Hearing"); *The Black Fly Review* ("Booming the Lake"); *The Bloomsbury Review* ("Annunciation"); *Western Humanities Review* (sections of "What Was So Beautiful About the Father").

The University of California, Irvine and the University of Utah supplied much support, financial and otherwise.

I would like to thank the Mary Anderson Center for time and support during the writing of this book. Also, thanks to Shireen and Reza Khazeni of the Reza Ali Khazeni Foundation for supplying faith and the wings for flight.

Note: In the poem "Grandfather," the excerpt of Ezekiel 1:22 is from the Hebrew Bible as translated by Jacqueline Osherow. The King James reads: "And the likeness of the firmament upon the heads of the living creature was as the color of the terrible crystal."